GEMSTONE POWER!

52 Meanings and Meditations from Abalone to Zircon

Harriette Knight

www.CharityClarityJewelry.com

Published by Charity Clarity Jewelry
© 2011 Harriette Knight

Printed in the United States of America

Knight, Harriette
    Gemstone Power! 52 Meanings and Meditations
        from Abalone to Zircon by Harriette Knight
ISBN-10: 0-9822427-2-7
ISBN-13: 978-0-9822427-2-8

To order, please call 661-254-4747 or visit
www.charityclarityjewelry.com.
Email inquiries to info@charityclarityjewelry.com

Cover design and layout by Dawn Teagarden.

Disclaimer - The purpose of this book is to educate and provide general information to support your quest for personal or spiritual growth. The author and publisher shall have neither liability or responsibility to anyone with respect to any loss or damage caused, or alleged to be caused, directly or indirectly by the information contained in this book, and are encouraged to seek professional assistance for all areas of healing.

This book is dedicated to Peaches,
who opened my heart in numerous ways.

ALSO BY HARRIETTE KNIGHT

CHAKRA POWER!
How to Fire Up Your Energy Centers to Live a Fuller Life

Easy Art from the Heart
A Rhyming Guidebook for Parents and Teachers

How to Fire Up Your Chakras
www.DailyOm.com

A Year of Intuitive Illuminations
www.DailyOm.com

Experience the Power of Gemstones
www.DailyOm.com

Harriette Knight's Psychic & Healing Hour
www.BlogTalkRadio.com/HarrietteKnight

Harriette Knight's YouTube Channel
www.YouTube.com/HarrietteKnight

Table of Contents

INTRODUCTION

I love stones. I love rocks. I love fossils. I love crystals. I love gemstones.

I love to work with them. I love to create with them. I love to display them.

As an artist, I utilize gemstones to make powerful pieces of jewelry that take on the healing attributes of the stones. As a healer, I then infuse the jewelry with healing energy that can help to support and stimulate a healthy body and spirit.

Working with gemstones and educating others about their healing qualities has changed my life. In my book *CHAKRA POWER! How to Fire Up Your Energy Centers to Live a Fuller Life,* I included a bonus section entitled Abalone to Zircon: The Meanings of the Stones You Wear. This popular addition to the book has now been expanded to include more details about the stones you love, and how they can help you. I've also included detailed definitions of numerous stones, plus a weekly life changing meditation that allows you to fully feel the effects of each one.

In *GEMSTONE POWER! 52 Meanings and Meditations from Abalone to Zircon* you will find everything you need to know about over 50 gemstones, their healing attributes, which chakras they affect, and how you can utilize them to change the course of your life. Whether you are adding to your own gemstone collection or looking for the perfect stone for a

friend or relative, this book will give you the tools to make excellent choices.

As a bonus, the meditations will prove life changing, as you embrace the power of each gemstone and integrate them into your own vibrational field. You will be amazed at how uplifting and renewed you will feel after reading each one. In addition, you will be given tips on how to clean and clear your gemstones so they can continue to serve you in the most positive way.

Gemstones are beautiful, natural, and have a life of their own. They can help you to heal, let go of old programming, enhance your intuition, and align your chakras. Gemstones add beauty to your surroundings, offset negative energy, and can be molded into gorgeous jewelry and artifacts. This easy to read handbook will show you firsthand how gemstones can change your life in a beautiful and positive way.

Experience the magical world of gemstones today!

Harriette Knight

MEDITATION GUIDELINES

With over 50 meditations in this book, you are now able to experience the true essence and vibration of each gemstone. Practicing the meditations consistently can help you to lift your spirit, move forward in your life, and bring you peace of mind.

You can utilize this book in many ways. Some will choose to read the book in order from A–Z, while others may pick and choose the stones they are drawn to. Holding the book and opening to any page is a great way to be guided to exactly what you need at the time. With enough weekly meditations to last for a whole year, you may choose to focus on just one stone per week before moving on to the next. Doing this can truly help you to mesh with the energy and integrate the qualities of the stone into your natural vibration.

By doing the meditation at the same time each day, your body, mind, and spirit will be ready and waiting. Doing something for 21 days can easily become a habit. Doing something for 28 days often turns into a lifestyle. Please remember to always do what feels comfortable and natural for you.

In the back of the book is a place for notes. Feel free to record your experiences from the meditations, what pages your favorite stones are on, or to simply make a list of stones you

would like to add to your collection. This is your book, and your personal journey. Embrace it!

For those just beginning their meditation practice, here is a wonderful routine for slowing down your breath to prepare for your meditation:

Sitting quietly, slow your breathing down by breathing in through your nose for four counts, hold for a count, then exhale through your nose for four counts. Hold for a count, and repeat for approximately three to four full breath cycles. When your breathing has slowed down to a comfortable rhythm, simply focus on the stone. If you have this gemstone in your personal collection, feel free to hold it.

GEMSTONES

1.
ABALONE

Abalone is a striking shell most often found in jewelry, decorative home accessories, and art. Though not officially considered a gemstone it does bring in all the elements from the sea including feeling calm and peaceful. Also known as Mother of Pearl, the iridescence of the inside of the shells reflects a rainbow of colors, which adds an extraordinary dimension to your gemstone collection. It helps to align the chakras, especially the heart. Because abalone comes from the ocean, it bears a strong connection to the moon and tides and enhances the Divine Feminine. Their shells are often used as a holder to burn sage bundles during house clearings and ceremonies. Adding to its versatility, abalone can be dyed most any color without losing any of its natural iridescence and shine.

ABALONE MEDITATION

Feel the calm of the sea and the natural movement of the water. Relax into a state of flow. Allow peace to wash over you. In and out. In and out. Just like the tide. Feel peace in your heart and let it radiate throughout your body in gentle waves. With each breath, your vibration takes on a shining glow that transforms into a rainbow of iridescent colors. Your aura is brighter, shinier, and glowing in the light of the sun and the moon. The waves of the sea flow in and out, and you feel renewed, refreshed, and at peace. The energy continues to flow effortlessly through each chakra, from the base of your spine up through the crown of your head. You are cleansed. You are beautiful. You are a shining, shining star.

2.
AGATE

A gate is an extraordinarily beautiful stone which comes in numerous colors and goes by many names such as Moss Agate and Blue Lace Agate. The most popular are polished stones and slices which resemble trunks of trees. This powerful stone promotes clarity, focus, and concentration. A memory booster, too! Agate is an excellent protection stone and is helpful for keeping one feel grounded and secure. Known as "The Stone of Balance," it can aid the healing of stomach issues including digestion and eating disorders. What begins in the mind is enhanced in the body, and with agate, the energy is multiplied. It is excellent for athletes and runners as it promotes agility and speed. This versatile stone is the official state gem of Louisiana, Maryland, Minnesota, Montana, Nebraska, and South Dakota.

AGATE MEDITATION

Feel the ground securely beneath your feet. Notice how locked in and connected to the earth you are. You are safe. You are protected. You are sure-footed. Nothing can topple you. Your strength is solid and purposeful. You are completely in balance, and feel peace within your core. Digestion is easy and uninterrupted. Your breathing is slow and steady. As you picture yourself moving forward, you can feel the ease of your legs carrying you. Slowly at first, but then picking up speed. Your muscles are strong and flexible. You are moving towards your destination. Each thought is clear and with purpose. Your memory comes back two fold, three fold, four fold. Your vision is like a laser as you see everything from your daily routine to your dreams and goals. You are carried with grace and ease, strength and focus. You are balanced. You are smart. You are successful.

3.
AMAZONITE

Amazonite is a beautiful turquoise stone with white inclusions. It supports the throat chakra as it assists in truthful and honest communication. Amazonite wards off negativity and is an excellent stone to keep by your computer to absorb the electronic waves. With the ability to help you sort through pertinent information, this is an excellent stone to use while researching. Not only will it help lead you to what you most need to know, it will help you retain the information. Held up to the forehead, your psychic ability is enhanced. Excellent for artists, too, as it opens the way for creativity. Amazonite assists the bones and teeth to stay strong since it also helps to absorb calcium. It promotes self confidence, friendly behavior and an ease to communicate effectively and effortlessly.

AMAZONITE MEDITATION

Visualize yourself in a social situation going from one person to the next and exchanging laughter and ideas. You feel friendly, lighter, and eager to connect with others. It's easy to communicate. You feel at ease in your body, and your words flow effortlessly as you exchange stories and quips. Sharing information is fun, and you know just what to say and how to say it. Confidence abounds and creative juices flow. Pulling ideas out of the air like plucking fruit from an abundant tree creates an eagerness to share thoughts and concepts through art and writing. Your workspace is clean and free from distraction. You are smart, strong, creative, and knowledgeable. Your smile is contagious.

4.
AMBER

Amber is the ultimate healing stone. Before there was penicillin, there was amber oil which was used to cure most everything. Dating back to the dinosaurs, amber is actually a sap that ranges in color from yellow to honey to green. It purifies and cleanses the aura, promotes balance, brings good luck, raises confidence levels and optimism, and supports your journey to enlightenment. It also aids healing in the areas of the stomach, gall bladder, kidneys, teeth, and joints. An excellent stone for supporting your Solar Plexus Chakra, amber can help turn up the heat for a low life force and give you an energy boost. Sometimes a bug or scorpion will be found inside an amber stone. This is often meant as lucky. Amber can be raw and rough, or shiny, and is a coveted stone for jewelry wearers.

AMBER MEDITATION

Picture a golden light in the center of your body. Feel it pulsating with each breath you take. Inhale, and exhale. Breathe even deeper and slower. Inhale, and exhale. Feel the light getting stronger and brighter. Inhale, and exhale. Treasure the breath. Inhale, and exhale. This golden light connects you to every single historical moment dating back to the beginning of time. You are at one with the earth. You are at one with mankind. You are part of every cell and being that has ever walked this planet. This golden light in your solar plexus continues to pulsate and become stronger and stronger, brighter and brighter until it radiates outward and fills your entire beingness with light. The warmth of the light, like sap, runs through your veins and fills you up from the middle of your core. You are healthy. You are strong. You are vibrant. You are joyful. You are LIFE.

5.
AMETHYST

Amethyst is the ultimate Royal Stone and an excellent tool for healing and meditation. It is the link between your human self and your spiritual side. Supporting your journey of faith and spirit, amethyst is used to enhance and open the Crown Chakra. It helps to control addictions, stimulate inspiration, and promote inner peace and honesty. This purple gem aids healing in the areas of the ears, bones, lungs, digestive system, respiratory tract, and skin. Encouraging sobriety, the Greeks lined wine goblets with this beautiful stone in the belief it would help keep one's head clear. It is no surprise that amethyst is also used to relieve headaches. This truly majestic stone is the birthstone for February, and the official state gem of South Carolina.

AMETHYST MEDITATION

The top of your head is wide open and surrounded by the brightest, whitest light you have ever seen. You can feel it fill the space above your head and radiate outward. Like a lighthouse beaming to the heavens. You are calling for a connection to Spirit, to the angels, to God. The connection is made at once, and your soul is filled with a warmth so pure, so loving, you might be moved to tears. This is love in its purest form. Your crown is now filled with a majestic purple hue, and if you listen closely you will hear the music of the Spheres. You are no longer human. You are entirely made up of light and love. A radiant vessel of spirit and soul. Your head is clear. You understand your purpose. You have been reunited with the most important part of your existence. Continue to feel the connection and relish the Oneness of God and Spirit and the Divine. You are love. You are light. You are radiant. You ARE.

6.
ANGELITE

Angelite is a soft blue and gentle stone that reminds us that the Angelic realm is very near. It encourages soft spoken communication between you and the loving beings that never leave your side. You are born with guardian angels who love you more than anything. Angelite opens the way for the connection to deepen, and the conscious, sub-conscious, and unconscious communication to flow effortlessly. A great stone for meditation, too. Your angels are ready and waiting to help you, however, you must first ask for their assistance. They cannot step in without being asked. Angelite allows for honesty and truthful communication. Use it often during your meditation practice and to soften the blow during confrontations. It can also be used to increase self love and forgiveness.

ANGELITE MEDITATION

Notice a soft breeze around your face. Could it be? A flurry of an angel wing? Yes, it is. Your spiritual helpers and guides flurry around your head. They gently kiss your brow and flutter through your hair. Your angels are giving thanks to you for allowing them to serve you. In return, embrace their presence. Bow your head in gratitude. Promise them that you will continue to rely on their goodness and kindness, and that you will ask them for help. They want to help you. They wait to help you. Ask them. The communication is easy and effortless. You are at one with your angels. You feel their love and warmth. You can see the glow radiating from their other worldliness. The connection through a silver tether can never be broken. You are in mutual reciprocity. Giving and receiving to one another. You are blessed. You are protected. You are loved.

7.
AQUAMARINE

Aquamarine is a stone of courage. It is a beautiful sea green; the color of both the sky and the water. It bodes well for sailors and is a good stone to pack when going on a cruise or boat ride. Fisherman find it lucky. This magical stone calls out to the mermaids for ease in breathing, and restoring calm and tranquility. It can help ward off sea sickness and promote balance especially during turbulent times. Use it as a peacemaker when you and your partner aren't seeing eye to eye. It can help ease communication between two parties and reactivate the natural flow of energy between you. Aquamarine can alleviate fears of the unknown, and can help remove past life trauma especially in regards to water. This March birthstone supports the throat chakra, and is the state gem of Colorado.

AQUAMARINE MEDITATION

You are lulled by the gentle motion of the sea as it rocks you back and forth. You feel soft. You feel safe. You feel connected to both the sky and the sea. There is no delineation between them. Just a solid hue of the most beautiful mix of blue and green you have ever seen. You feel a catch in your throat as your heart opens to such beauty. You can stay like this forever. Floating. The sky, the sea, and you. You continue to rock gently. All fears are assuaged and wash away. There is nothing but peace and calm, and the soft sounds of mermaids as they bob up to check on you. You are safe. You are balanced. Nothing weighs heavily on your chest. You can breathe with ease. You can travel safely. You are fully protected. You can float like this forever. You are, and always will be, fully at peace.

8.
ARAGONITE

Aragonite is a grounding stone with crystal vines bursting from its core. It is named after the place it was first discovered, Aragon, in Spain. It is an anchor for the root chakra fortifying your connection to the earth. Strength, security, overcoming sadness and sensitivity are attributes of this reddish/brown gem. Aragonite can be used to help pull you out of a funk when times get too rough. It can boost your confidence and remind you of your true purpose. Use it during meditation to help whittle away what no longer serves you so you can move forward on your path. This is a strong stone associated with the characteristics of Capricorn. Success, discipline, focus, and the ability to maintain continuity between who you are, who you were, and who you strive to be. Aragonite also aids in the absorption of calcium for strong teeth and bones.

ARAGONITE MEDITATION

There is a rumble underneath your feet. Don't worry. You are safe and secure. The rumbling is your confidence as it bubbles up to the surface for the next part of your journey. You can remember your past. You are aware of your present. Your future awaits. The decks are clearing. You are strong and protected. Grounded into the earth. You are secure and focused. Confident and sure-footed. No hill seems too large. No task, insurmountable. You are ready to move forward with ease. Your body is strong. There is no pain. No fear. No sadness. Only the truth of who you are, and what you can accomplish. Anchor your goals into the earth. Allow them to grow strong and surpass your wildest imagination. The rumbling you feel is your confidence bursting with pride. You are achieving, and there is no holding you back!

9.
ATLANTISITE

Atlantisite is a combination of Serpentine and Stichtite. It is a mottled green stone with purple spots and specks. This stone allows you to retrieve the codes of the past, and help you to remember the knowledge of lost civilizations so it can be healed on an ethereal level. Atlantisite will help you align your entire chakra system, giving a boost to your kundalini (life force) and utilizing the energy for a spiritual boost. This stone helps to right past wrongs, and allows you to see the lessons learned so they will never occur again. It will connect you to higher knowledge and give you the ability to channel information in a clear and concise way. This is a stone of re-generation. What once was lost, can live again, in truth and honor, and for the betterment of all beings on this planet and beyond.

ATLANTISITE MEDITATION

Deep in the channels of past programming, you sense a familiarity. A knowledge of a time that was forced to end. This is a time of grief and confusion. Pulling yourself out of that confusion, you leave it behind forever. This is a time of forgiveness. A time to utilize important knowledge for the greater good of ALL. You feel a stirring in your root chakra as your kundalini is released. You are empowered to do what is good and right. It is an epiphany of knowledge. Of understanding. You see codes and messages, and the meaning of all civilization. You are fully present, and can now put the past to rest once and for all. You are at peace. You are knowledgeable. You are in complete harmony with the past, the present, and the future. You have healed old wounds so peace can prevail. You feel empowered, and grateful. There is no remorse. No guilt. You are free.

10.
AVENTURINE

Aventurine is a wonderful green stone supporting love and money! It promotes growth, abundance, prosperity, optimism, and recovery. Aventurine supports the heart chakra and any ailments that reside there. It encourages regeneration, helps to lower cholesterol, heals the skin, and alleviates pain and allergies. It is an excellent stone for anyone in the healing profession including doctors, nurses, and the clergy since it opens the way for compassion. For relief from fevers, skin ailments, or heartache, put your aventurine gemstone in your bath water. This all around healing stone also comes in a red tone.

AVENTURINE MEDITATION

Feel the welling up in your heart chakra. It is pulsating with pure optimism. You are ready for all abundance to flow into your life with ease. Love, money, security, and joy are settling into your heart for your entire lifetime. Your heart fills with gratitude and compassion. You are so abundant you can now help others in need. There is an explosion of prosperity and it is received with open arms. There is so much joy, you can't stop the laughter from erupting from your lips. You feel full, satisfied, and ready to hug the world. Love is here to stay. Abundance of good health and well-being is yours. You are calm and free from worry. No more stress. No more fear. You are giving. You are receiving.

11.
CARNELIAN

Carnelian is a power stone and a protection stone. It can help pull you out of a rut by promoting action and courage. It helps to stop confusion, lift your emotions, and protect you from fear and envy. Carnelian can fuel your passions by encouraging you to choose the right career path. As it energizes your personal power center, it also cleanses and purifies your sacral chakra, soothes menstrual cramps, supports kidney function, and helps battle infertility. A must for your stone collection, this powerhouse ranges in color from light red to deep brown, and helps to stimulate the absorption of vitamins. Use it for decision making, empowerment, releasing anger and rage, and uncovering your hidden talents. This rich stone is great for confidence and self esteem, releasing fear, and tapping into your most primal nature.

GEMSTONE POWER!

CARNELIAN MEDITATION

Tap into your personal power source by plugging in to your sacral chakra which is two inches below your belly button. Picture the color orange as it vacillates between darker and lighter hues. As the flow of energy fills you up, anger, rage, and emptiness are easily released. You are a living breathing human, and with a rush of energy, you are at once focused and excited. You emerge mighty and powerful, protected by your guides who are leading you by the hand to find your true purpose. You connect with your passions and release any ties to those who have hurt or disappointed you in the past. When letting go, you feel another rush of energy signifying new life. You can feel it stirring in your belly as you begin anew. You feel conviction and pride. Wholeness and courage. Your head is high. You walk tall. You are powerful. You are strong. You are free.

12.
CHRYSOCOLLA

Chrysocolla is a green stone that is often mistaken for turquoise. It is soothing and relaxing, promotes patience and understanding, encourages clarity and perception, and helps to deal with sudden and unexpected changes in our lives. It is excellent for healing infections pertaining to the throat and tonsils, but also helps with digestion, liver function, and lowering blood pressure. It can be used daily for keeping you feel calm, relaxed, and in general good health. Because of this calming attribute, you may find yourself more open to expressing yourself creatively and compassionately. A great tool for artists and writers who suffer from artistic blockages, too!

CHRYSOCOLLA MEDITATION

All at once you feel an intense calm. Your throat relaxes. Your brow relaxes. Your heart opens. You feel quiet and patient, as if you have all the time in the world. Everything in your life appears smooth with no rough edges. Your heartbeat slows, and you are able to take a breath. And then another one. Calm. Patient. Relaxed. Out of this stillness comes the beginning of an idea. Like a beacon of light it comes into focus. Your creativity is sparked and you have a sense that this is the answer you've been looking for. A new way of looking at an old situation. You feel peaceful and renewed. You release the old, and approach the rest of your life in a profoundly new and compassionate way. A gentle beginning of a smile on your lips, you are calm and ready, creative and thriving, joyous and peaceful.

13.
CITRINE

Citrine is THE manifestation stone. A stone of good luck, prosperity, and confidence. As it lifts the spirit, it encourages mental and emotional clarity and well being. This yellow stone supports the Solar Plexus Chakra and gives a boost to your life force. It is so powerful, it never absorbs any negativity. Because of this, you will not have to clean or clear it. Citrine helps optimize memory, understanding, recovery from addictions, and self-growth. It encourages hopes and dreams, willpower, and higher self-esteem. Citrine can be helpful to those who suffer from depression during the long winter months since it brings in energy from the sun. In addition, it is beneficial to those with eating disorders, stomach and bladder problems, and diabetes.

CITRINE MEDITATION

Notice a small light in the center of your body. Like a pilot light that is always on, it glows. The light grows brighter and brighter as you turn up the flame. This is your life force, and your will to live. The golden yellow light fills your entire frame dispelling doubt, depression, and insecurity. You can feel the boost of confidence as you gain clarity and focus of what you want and deserve. Your hopes and dreams become fleshed out and you can see and feel abundance, prosperity, luck, and good fortune. You CAN have it all. You DESERVE to have it all. You WILL have it all. Your life force is shining, and nothing can stop you now.

14.
EMERALD

Emerald is the stone of Prosperity and Riches. It supports your Heart Chakra and helps to bring in what you truly desire. It is a romantic stone, with many brides choosing it over a diamond. Inspiration, clairvoyance, sensuality, love, beauty, harmony, friendship, and unity are all highlighted by this stone's properties. This brilliant green gemstone aids healing in the areas of the upper respiratory tract, the heart, and the eyes. As it detoxifies the body, it also helps build up the immune system. A state known for its lush greenery, North Carolina, boasts the emerald as its official state gem, and those born in the month of May claim it as their birthstone.

EMERALD MEDITATION

Your chest swells with pride with each breath you take. Your Heart Chakra fills up with a sense of security, prosperity, and love for others. You are regal. You stand tall and confident. Your gift of foresight allows others to look to you for guidance. You embrace this role with ease. You are a leader and a healer, and have been for many lifetimes. Riches pour into your life from unknown sources. People love to give you money. You are rewarded over and over for your many gifts. You are gracious and loving and accepting. You are honored and recognized many times over. You have the innate ability to see what others aren't able to see for themselves. With grace and ease you are there to help, and are rewarded handsomely. You are proud. You are rich. You are successful.

15.
FLUORITE

Fluorite comes in a variety of colors with the most popular being clear, purple, green, and blue. This magical stone helps open up the subconscious mind to be more receptive to angelic messages. Use it while meditating and begin to listen to your creative muses. Fluorite inspires, and helps to free self imposed restrictions. As your self confidence increases, so will your awareness. Like agate and carnelian, fluorite boosts mental concentration which is why it is a favorite for students. It fortifies teeth and bones, helps the skin to regenerate, keeps the body strong and healthy, improves posture, and repels upper respiratory infections and allergies. This powerhouse is the official state mineral of Illinois.

FLUORITE MEDITATION

As the universal light flows in through the top of your head, your Third Eye Chakra is wide open. You are intuitive and can feel information flowing effortlessly from your subconscious to your conscious mind. Sharp, clear images rush to the forefront. You are engaged and stimulated intellectually and creatively. Your muses offer an assortment of ideas and techniques which are tangible and accessible. You sense a flutter of activity as your angelic team gathers around you for support. You are never alone and feel their presence 24 hours a day. With the support of your universal team, nothing holds you back. You are intuitive. You are connected. You are inspired. You see all. You know all. You are ALL.

16.
FOSSILIZED
WOOD

Fossilized Wood is usually found in earth tones of browns and reds. It is also known as Petrified Wood. As the wood petrifies, it takes on a gemstone quality that is magnificent. It encourages new beginnings, calms you down, and aids in recovery. Fossilized wood helps keep you grounded, and since it stimulates the metabolism, it is an excellent stone for dieting and stress. Associated with the Root Chakra, this gemstone helps to sow your dreams into an abundant harvest by planting them deep within the earth. As the idea, concept, or dream takes root, it is encouraged to grow into a strong and sturdy reality. The State of Washington has adopted this stone as its official gem.

FOSSILIZED WOOD MEDITATION

Connecting with your Root Chakra at the base of your spine, you anchor yourself. Feel strong and sturdy. The energy from your Root Chakra reaches down into the earth and supports you. The earth is rich and dark and full of resources to nurture your dreams and goals. Focus on what you want. If you don't know, ask for assistance to define the perfect goal for you. Take the seed of your dream and plant it into the earth below you. Send lots of light and love to foster strength, good health, and support. Understand fully that your goal is growing into a reality. It is securing your future so that you will remain strong and never topple. You are anchored. You are supported. You are branching out.

17.
GARNET

Garnet is a power stone and the birthstone for those born in January. It fires up the Root Chakra as it rules sexuality, passion, prosperity, and new beginnings. This stone is usually red in color but can also be green, black, pink, orange, and yellow. It addresses the Divine Feminine, and helps to eliminate emotional blockages and inspire romantic love. It aids in cell regeneration, boosts the immune system, helps with arthritis and strengthens bones. Garnet can also accelerate wound healing and works as an anti-inflammatory. It is an excellent stone to have when moving to a new location or changing jobs as it brings out your best qualities so you can attract new friends, associates, and like-minded individuals. It is the official state gem of Idaho (Star Garnet), New York (Almandine Garnet), and Vermont (Grossular Garnet).

GARNET MEDITATION

Ask yourself, who would you be, if you had no past? Would you be wildly passionate, exciting, successful, and self-confident? You already are! Feel the passion as it stirs you to greatness. Unzip yourself out of that worn out coat, and see yourself in something new, something vibrant, something red. Everywhere you go, heads turn. You have friends in all the right places. You attract high energy, like-minded people. You have the wherewithal to get where you want to go and the resources to take you there in style. You are exuberant and full of resounding energy. You smolder during the day and sizzle at night. You are wooed by romance, and wowed by sensuality. You are hot. You are sexy. You are wildly successful. You are fabulous.

18.
HEMATITE

Hematite is also referred to as Bloodstone and helps with circulation and iron absorption. As it improves the oxygen supply to your body, you can enjoy greater health, sleep soundly at night, and have more vitality and energy during the day. This stone looks like metal with its shiny gray and silver tone. It is excellent for mind control, and exceptional for those who work with computers. It is often paired with magnets and made into necklaces, bracelets, and anklets to encourage better circulation and spine alignment. Those with cold hands and feet may find some relief while wearing hematite as it opens the way for the blood to flow with ease. It also helps to reduce cholesterol and dissolve negativity. Alabama and New York have made Hematite their official state mineral.

HEMATITE MEDITATION

Connecting with your heart, feel it pumping your life force through your veins. Circulating healthy cells, iron rich blood, and vitality in a never ending cycle of rhythm and flow. Everything inside you is in a constant state of motion as it warms and nurtures you. Your organs are in sync with your breathing. Your blood flow is rich and cleansing. Your mind is sharp and focused. There is no negativity. Only Oneness. You are everything. You are your liver, your lungs, your heart. You are your skin, your bones, your joints. You are complete and perfect. Your spine is strong. You radiate health. You have color in your cheeks, warm hands, warm feet, and the warmest heart. You are ready to solve all of life's riddles. You are sharp. You are quick. You are in sync.

19.
HOWLITE

Howlite is a calming white stone with gray veins that can be dyed most any color. It is not a surprise to see neon green, turquoise, or hot pink howlite used in fashionable jewelry. The veins signify reaching for your dreams and goals. Some of the veins are direct and clear, while others fan out in numerous directions. This relaxing and loving stone helps absorb stress and anxiety. Since it works well to quiet the mind, it is often used for those who suffer from insomnia. Howlite helps to dispel selfishness, let go of anger, and diffuse confrontations. On a practical level, it is an excellent stone to assist you in balancing your calcium levels and strengthening your teeth and bones.

HOWLITE MEDITATION

Breathe. A slow, quiet, and gentle breath. You feel calm. Relaxed. Not a care or worry in the world. You are so light, you feel as if you could float up, up, up, and connect directly with Source. You are breathing freely and entering a dream state where anything is possible. It is effortless. You are loved. Supported by the universe. Calm. There is not an angry bone in your body. All worries have vanished. You are a clean slate where your deepest wishes and dreams are written. The past is erased. Your future is bright. There is no anger. No fear. You are relaxed. You are calm. You are loved.

20.
JADE

Jade is a sacred stone that has been around for centuries. It is a stone of good fortune, wealth, prosperity and luck. Jade brings about inner peace and awareness, promotes self realization, and can keep you on track towards your dreams and goals. Ruling the Heart Chakra, green jade can reduce emotional and mental stress and encourage honesty. It may also improve agility and muscle responses. Many believe that jade helps one to express love more easily and can be used to enhance lovemaking. Keeping a piece of jade under your pillow has been known to help you to remember your dreams, and then turn those dreams into a reality. This rich stone can be intricately carved into most anything such as buddhas, dragons, bonsai trees, and any type of jewelry. It ranges in color from green to red to orange to yellow to pink to black to white, and is the official state gem of Wyoming.

JADE MEDITATION

Picture riches falling from the sky. Blessings coming to you in bulk. Prosperity and good fortune is falling into your arms. You are grateful. Your heart opens up in a surge of gratitude and love for all mankind. You are in perfect balance and all your needs are being met. You feel a sense of peace and tranquility knowing that you will never have to worry about material wealth again. It is all yours. You have deep wisdom and courage to use this wealth wisely. It comes in many forms, but always abundant. You are lucky in love, career, and relationships. You are generous and humble, compassionate and wise. You understand your place in the world and your connection to spirituality. You radiate health and will live a long and prosperous life. Your heart is open. You are loved. You are vibrant. You are lucky. You are happy.

21.
JASPER

Jasper goes by many names such as Red Jasper, Picture Jasper, Leopardskin Jasper, and Ocean Jasper. It is a powerful stone that is excellent for protection and grounding. It comes in an assortment of colors and natural designs. Picture Jasper often looks like a photograph of a painted desert or mountain against a blue sky, while other specimens look like pen and ink etchings. All jasper stones promote courage and strength, stability and willpower, and reduce stress and conflicts. Jasper can help to alleviate flu symptoms, indigestion, and intestinal difficulties. Once known as "The Warrior Stone," jasper can help to boost confidence, and allow for fair play. It offers a slow and steady approach to change which is helpful to those who prefer a less dramatic environment.

JASPER MEDITATION

You feel solid. Strong. Like a rock. Secure. You feel confident and courageous. You know what you want, and it comes to you effortlessly. There is no conflict, only peace. You are strong, secure, and stabile. You have a sense that everything is in order, and it is. You have come a long way in your life, fought many battles, and now you feel independent and strong. Everything is as it should be. You are a warrior. Slow and steady and discerning. You are on track, clear headed, and nothing can rock your stance. You are strong. You are grounded. You are protected.

22.
KYANITE

Kyanite, like Citrine, is a stone that is unable to absorb negativity so it never needs cleaning or clearing. It is a powerful stone that aligns all the chakras, and opens up the psychic channels for clearer intuition and meditation. It promotes honest communication, vivid dreaming, and loyalty. Using kyanite to turn your dreams into reality is helpful. It is a powerful, yet calming stone, and allows the nature of events to unfold effortlessly. A Third Eye activator, kyanite is often used to access channeled information. It is an excellent stone for those who have a hard time sitting still whether it's due to their natural energy levels or during meditation. Kyanite allows for a more direct communication between thinking and speaking, and is helpful for those who struggle with admitting the truth.

KYANITE MEDITATION

You might notice a chill as your chakras are immediately aligned. You feel balanced and calm. Anxiety is released. No need to fidget. Be still, and breathe. Allow yourself to sit in the energy and remain open to the download of information that comes from Source. You are able to focus and resolve an inner struggle that has gone on far too long. You find it easy to be in this meditative state, and are open to what comes next. Your thought process is changing. You have a better understanding of who you are, and how to communicate from within your true authentic self. Guided by the information that comes through your dreams, you are able to make decisions with ease. Communication is effortless between you, Source, and others. You are clear. You are honest. You are truthful.

23.
LABRADORITE

Labradorite is a magical stone. It has a gorgeous iridescence in blues and greens that come to life in the light. Labradorite is so magical it enhances mediumistic abilities, and heightens intuition. It is a powerful yet calming stone, and opens the way for empathic behavior. Labradorite helps to lower blood pressure, keep colds away, and enhance self-esteem. It can help to open the way for a clearer vision of what has remained hidden. In fact, labradorite enhances all vision; that of the eyes and the Third Eye. With the help of labradorite, psychic information that comes through your dreams can be used to hone your natural abilities, and make it easier to share your gifts with the world. With its intricate detail of light, shine, and magic, labradorite is a favorite to use as a meditation tool.

LABRADORITE MEDITATION

What you notice first is how clear your vision is. Crystal clear. You have thought upon thought and it comes in waves of clarity. Your eyes are more focused, and even in the night, your visibility is enhanced. It's as if the windshield of your mind has cleared and you can effortlessly see and feel what is and has been in front of you all along. You can tune in effortlessly to the thoughts and feelings of those around you. You connect on a deeper level to your dreams which spill out knowledge and information to help you broaden your capabilities. Your confidence increases as you utilize your new found mediumship to connect with all that is, all that was, and all that shall be. You honor your skills, and use these them wisely. You are bright. You are smart. You are an open channel. You can effortlessly see ALL.

24.
LAPIS LAZULI

Lapis Lazuli is a deep blue stone that enhances honest communication. Since it aids healing in the areas of the neck, vocal chords, and larynx, it is a perfect stone to wear as a necklace. A fifth and sixth chakra enhancement, this powerful stone is also ruled by mercury. Mercury is the planet of communication. The fifth chakra is the Throat Chakra, also denoting communication. Communication, communication, communication! Lapis is a stone of friendship, abundance, and helps to enhance psychic communication, not only with others but with that part of yourself that is connected to the ALL. It can also help pull you out of a funk, as it is a natural antidote for depression. Opening the way for complete honesty, lapis lazuli helps you to become "true blue" in friendships, relationships, and the ability to fearlessly speak your mind without confrontation.

LAPIS LAZULI MEDITATION

You might notice a stirring in your throat as it opens the way for easier breathing. Speaking is effortless and words seem to flow in a loving and honest way. There is no judgement, only truth, and the desire to communicate becomes overwhelming and exciting. There is no holding back. You are free to say what you want effortlessly and easily. You feel safe, and secure. As the channel opens between your Third Eye and Throat Chakra, you are able to let go and communicate your deepest thoughts and desires. It's as if a restriction or constriction has been lifted for the first and last time. There is no more holding back as words flow out of your heart into your head and out your lips. A beautiful triumvirate of light, love, communication, and song.

25.
LEMURIAN SEED

Lemurian seeds are crystals of the highest vibration. They stem from Lemuria, a civilization that existed at the time of Atlantis. Lemuria was a land of total peace and democracy. There was no war, and no hardship. Nature played an integral part in the lifestyle of the Lemurians. They were of the highest consciousness, extremely psychic, and loving. Lemurian seeds have ridges on the sides of the crystals known as record keepers. This is sacred knowledge of the past and allows for direct communication with the spirit world. You may notice, too, that there are triangles naturally carved into the crystals. These hold information for the future, which is helpful for conscious dreaming and healing. This very loving stone is excellent for meditation, aligning the chakras, and connecting with other stars and galaxies.

LEMURIAN SEED MEDITATION

You are simply at peace. And, love radiates through every cell; every ounce of your being. You are all knowing, and instantly connect to the Akashic records that hold the answers of the universe. You are at one with Spirit, your guides, your angels, and the planet. You are all knowing. All loving. All peaceful. There is no beginning and no end to this enormous feeling of connectivity. From the deepest part of your heart, you understand that all karmic debt has been paid. You experience eternal peace of mind, and see the light in each and every one of us. As you take a breath, your entire chakra system is aligned and lit. You connect with ease to the vastness of the dream world, gaining knowledge that can help heal yourself and others. You are One. You are purity. You are the embodiment of peace and love. You ARE.

26.
MALACHITE

Malachite is a brilliant green stone with lots of detail. It promotes willpower, desire, friendship, determination, and helps to overcome shyness. It is associated with the Heart Chakra. Malachite is an excellent protection stone for children that helps during transitional times. It is used to alleviate mental blockages, assuage guilt, and allow for anxiety and resentment to be released. Malachite is especially helpful when you are ready to let go of the past and move forward into your true authentic self. It is a stone to assist you to let go of what no longer serves you, and allow for changes to come swiftly and easily. This bright green stone can help to ease conflicts in all types of relationships including business. A helpful stone for fear of flying, it is a favorite for pilots and travelers. If you are drawn to malachite, good luck is on its way.

MALACHITE MEDITATION

With each breath you can feel pieces of the past falling away. It is effortless. Even memories that are buried too deep to remember are released with ease. You are letting go of the past and moving forward into your future. No more shyness. No more guilt. You are protected during this transitional time and feel as safe as a child in their parent's loving arms. Your heart is full as you realize that you can achieve what you want, and deserve to be rewarded. There are no blockages, only smooth sailing ahead. Your heart is open. You are soaring freely. You are successful. Harmonious. Inner and outer conflicts are put to rest for good. You are free to move forward, and supported every step of the way. You are flying high. Flying strong. Flying freely.

27.
MOONSTONE

Moonstone is a must when celebrating the Divine Feminine. Even if you are a man. It is a white stone with a bluish shimmer that is known to increase clairvoyance and depth of love. As it aligns your emotional self with your higher self, moonstone can bring in more lucid dreaming and better intuition. This balancing stone brings in good fortune for both men and women. It is a lucky stone for travelers and business owners. Moonstone helps to create and nurture a bountiful garden. Many choose to carry it in their pocket to balance their emotions, bring love into their lives, or patch up quarrels with loved ones. It is often a gift for those embarking on the road to motherhood, as it enhances fertility and balances hormones. It is excellent for those in the medical and therapeutic profession since it instills compassion and empathy towards others without judgement. This magical stone is the state gem of Florida, which is the home of the Fountain of Youth.

MOONSTONE MEDITATION

Center yourself. Breathe in the yin. Gently release. And now, breathe in the yang. Feel the energy. You are both feminine and masculine. You are open to the flow of energy as it spreads through your body. Embarking on your journey, you feel protected and guided. Luck finds you and follows you. You feel a quiver of new life whether it is a new baby, a new idea, a new business venture. You are fertile and lucid. Balanced and compassionate. Your travels are vast and span a lifetime. You are always protected. By the light of the moon, you find your way. Mother Earth provides sustenance and nourishment to your soul. You reap the benefits by giving gratitude. To the moon. To the earth. To the Great Mother in us all.

28.
ONYX

Onyx is an excellent stone for concentration, focus, grounding, and confidence. It helps to stimulate logical communication, and sharpen your sense of hearing. Onyx helps put you in charge of your own fate and is a favorite for entrepreneurs and inventors. It helps stimulate the mind to bring forth new and practical ideas. With onyx, you will not be influenced by other people's negativity. It's a sobering stone; not frivolous. If you are serious about a task, onyx will aid you to keep on it until completed. It can help let go of past relationships or thought patterns that no longer serve you. Associated with the Root Chakra, this stone will help keep you steadfast and strong without emotional drama. Though most popular in black, onyx actually comes in a variety of colors including red, green, and white.

ONYX MEDITATION

As your breathing slows, you sense a shift in energy. You are focused, and on your path. There are no distractions, only the task at hand. You are motivated to finish what you have started out to do, and check things off your list. You can already feel a sense of accomplishment, knowing everything will unfold as it should. You are clear, and able to concentrate without distraction, without negativity, without a blow to the ego. You are strong and in control of your future. Your destiny is carved in stone and all you have to do is step on the conveyor belt of clarity to take you there. You focus only on the positive and are able to think out of the box to come up with a great plan. You have foresight to know what is best for all concerned. You are serious. You are not to be stopped. You are listening for the cues. You are moving forward. You are purposeful.

29.
OPAL

Opal is the magical stone of October births. It gives you the will to live, to love, and to experience joy! Opal enhances desire, sexuality, even eroticism. It is the stone for the Scorpio in all of us, ruling the Sacral Chakra, the sexual organs, and creating fire in your life force. There is an old wives tale that believes that only those born in October should wear an opal. THIS IS NOT TRUE!! Opal is a gorgeous white stone with every color of the rainbow woven through its iridescence. It helps to relieve tension and anxiety, and bestows angelic dreams and harmony. It is a great stone for healing, and instills a sense of hope and accomplishment. A protection stone, opal can attune to both negative and positive energy, weeding out one from the other. It is the original "Evil Eye" which protects against harm. Opals have often come with a warning for those in love, for it is believed that an opal will bring misfortune to one who strays. Stay faithful, stay true, and stay above board to reap all the benefits this stone has to offer.

OPAL MEDITATION

You first feel the spark in your belly, like a quickening of life. It feels good, and exciting. Like a heat lamp warming up. You feel the fire as it spreads throughout your body. Your groin. Your stomach. Your heart. Your head. You are on fire and it feels magnificent. Your inner iridescence cannot contain itself another minute. Your eyes light up like beams of light as you connect to your innermost vibration. You are love. You are in love. You are part of love. You are the eternal love. You make a pact with yourself to continue to shine and spread the wingspan of your lifeline to above and beyond. The fire spreads beyond your aura to connect with the music of the Spheres. There is no darkness, only light. There is hope, and feelings of oneness between you and all of mankind and universe. You give life. You receive life. You are life. You are RADIANT.

30.
PEARL

Pearl is a symbol of a pure heart, and carries an innocence that is very soothing. It promotes faith, charity, and balances emotions especially for those born under the water signs of Cancer, Scorpio, and Pisces. Pearl is the oldest known gem and for centuries was deemed as the most valuable. It was once called "Teardrops from the Moon," since it was believed that pearls were formed from a single raindrop that became the heart of the oyster. Wearing pearls may help to increase fertility and decrease acid indigestion. They can remind you to walk with dignity and maintain a sense of self. Though most commonly white in color, pearls can be dyed to take on any hue. They can make you feel beautiful and ultra-feminine. Perhaps this is why so many brides choose to wear them on their wedding day. Since June is a popular wedding month, it is no surprise that pearls are also June's birthstone. This gentle stone is the official state gem of Kentucky and Tennessee.

PEARL MEDITATION

As you look towards the heavens you see a single drop of dew fall from the sky. This drop of dew takes up residence inside your heart and grows into purity, charity, and innocence. Your eyes are clear, and you see the world as if for the very first time. You are mesmerized by the prisms of light that come off the tips of the sea, or leaves kissed by the rain. There is an awareness that you are part of something special and loving. This immediately calms you, and you are moved to hold your head high and proceed with new eyes and an innocent heart towards the light of your future. A new dawn. A new day. A new life. Starting fresh, you write your story on undisturbed sand; the waves lapping at the shore, the peace in your heart. Your story is protected and cherished. It is yours and yours alone, to be shared only by those who cherish you in return.

31.
PERIDOT

Peridot is a lovely green or yellow stone supporting the Heart and Solar Plexus chakras. It helps to rejuvenate and restore your life force. Peridot can assist you to get back on your feet after a bout of low self confidence. It is especially helpful for those who want to move past heartache, and gain objectivity in regard to love and relationships. This August birthstone promotes independence, prosperity, personal growth, and a zest for life. It is excellent for forgiveness and releasing anger. Peridot aids healing in the area of the liver as it stimulates metabolism and helps to detox the system. Good for warts and skin ailments, too. Peridot is a money stone and opens the way for prosperity to come your way. Use it in conjunction with citrine, which will help you keep the money once you get it!

PERIDOT MEDITATION

Breathe in. Fill your Heart Chakra with forgiveness, and let it warm your body. There is no anger. There is no pain. Feel yourself rise up above so you can look down at yourself objectively, and see the brilliant golden light that is you. There is no jealousy. There is no fear. As you remain perched above yourself, envision money and love flowing your way. Notice how you embrace these riches and your golden light gets brighter and brighter. You are deserving of all good things. The darkness abates. The sadness is gone. There is only light and love and utter joy. As you merge back into your body, you feel independent and strong. You understand that the past is long gone, and you have everything you need to live in a world full of abundance, prosperity, good health, and happiness. You are motivated. You are active. You are joyful.

32.
PYRITE

Pyrite is also known as "Fool's Gold," but there is nothing foolish about it. It supports the Solar Plexus chakra, and helps to shield you from negativity. Keeping a piece of pyrite on your desk can help you overcome procrastination. It is a stone of good luck and just like gold, prosperity. Pyrite is much harder than gold and cannot be bent or molded. In fact, if stricken by steel, the stone would spark. Pyrite actually means 'Stone of Fire,' and got its name from the Greeks. It can energize a low metabolism, and help you overcome fatigue. It supports the lungs, and may help those who suffer from asthma. As it energizes your body, your circulatory system will improve, giving you strength and stamina.

PYRITE MEDITATION

Feel the fire in your belly as it warms your soul. You are bright and energized, and ready to take on the world. Positivity and optimism abound. You feel strong, and your lungs fill completely with health and longevity. Breathing is so easy, you do it again and again, filling your body completely with clean and clear prana. Prana, your life force, is hard to contain. You want to run; miles and miles, bringing you closer to your goals. There is no time like the present. You are ready to go. You are strong and flexible. Your personal fire has been sparked and there is no snuffing it out. It continues to grow into a bonfire of good health, strength, confidence, and stamina. You can't contain the light even if you tried. You simply shine, shine, shine, SHINE!

33.
QUARTZ
CRYSTAL

Quartz Crystal is THE MOST POWERFUL HEALING STONE. It aligns all the chakras, and brings about clarity, focus, and connection to one's Higher Self. It amplifies the energy of all other stones, and brings about spiritual healing, peace, intuition, creativity, balance, perceptiveness, and understanding. Quartz crystals can help find what was lost, whether in a material or an emotional sense. It helps to dispel negativity and depression, and to solve problems. For those who often feel cold or experience numbness, quartz crystal may be a perfect antidote. It helps to balance the yin and yang of the brain by supplying energy where it is most needed. This is an excellent tool for meditation as it opens up the crown chakra and taps into Universal Law. It raises your vibration so you can be fully present on your personal path, and brings in clarity, focus, and peace of mind. A must for your stone collection! This conductor of energy is the official state gem of Georgia.

QUARTZ CRYSTAL MEDITATION

You can feel it right away. A buzzing that starts off as a low hum. It resonates to your personal vibration, and your chakras are aligned one by one. First, your root chakra at the base of your spine. You feel empowered. And, strong. Moving up to your sacral, the buzzing continues and stirs something in your belly. You feel creative, and find yourself smiling. Your solar plexus feels energized and the buzzing gets stronger. You understand that leaving your mark on the world is not an option. You become clear and focused. Your heart chakra fills to the brim with pride. You radiate love to the world. It's all crystal clear now, and you understand that you are connected to every being on the planet. Your throat chakra fills with the vibration, and you are ready to communicate and voice your presence. Your whole body vibrates as your third eye opens and with crystal clarity you can see the past, present, and future. It is rich and abundant. As you are filled with light, your crown chakra connects to the heavens and ALL THAT IS. Your spirit guides, angels, and Masters guide you to your future. As the buzzing subsides you are left feeling peaceful, calm, present, and never alone. You are clear. You are positive. You are the best that you can be.

34.
RHODOCHROSITE

Rhodochrosite is a brilliant raspberry stone; the color as rich as Hawaiian Punch. It has the ability to make you feel happy, bring about enthusiasm, and maintain a positive attitude. Rhodochrosite encourages you to be playful, even in a sexual way. It can help with circulation, blood pressure, kidney and joint problems, and may ease migraines. Rhodochrosite has been known to help bring in the perfect soulmate for your personal and spiritual growth. Your "twin soul" may not be who you think it is. Rhodochrosite can open the way for the perfect person to come along so you can learn what you most need to know. It has the ability to help those who are unable to feel love in their heart, and open the Heart Chakra to receive love from others. Rhodochrosite can deflect negativity, lift your spirits, and allow you to see the truth about who you really are, in a loving and positive way.

RHODOCHROSITE MEDITATION

Immediately you feel the fog lift, and all heaviness disappears. You feel lighter and brighter, and your heart bursts with joy. You feel playful, and long to have fun, hear a joke, run, and laugh in the wind. You've returned to that place in your heart that is innocent and secure. Quite simply, you feel loved. There is no emotional baggage, only joy and humor and fun. You visualize someone next to you. A mirror image, a soulmate, a twin. Someone who knows you better than anybody else. You are reminded of first loves and first kisses. You can't help but smile, and embrace the moment. A time of fun. Frivolity. Fantasy. You can be anyone and anything you want. You embrace your oneness, and long to share it with the world. Your heart is open. You receive with grace. You are loved. You are happy. You are bursting with joy!

35.
RHODONITE

Rhodonite is a pink healing stone with gray and black veins. It can encourage forgiveness, friendship, and bring love and passion into action. For self confidence, spiritual maturity, and the ability to let go of unwanted behaviors, rhodonite is a great tool. It can balance your personal yin and yang, give your internal love light a boost, and calm you down during a crisis. The official state gem of Massachusetts, rhodonite supports the Sacral and Heart chakras. It can ease traumas of the past, heal a broken heart, and stimulate fertility. Rhodonite is helpful to those who are being treated for lung and breathing disorders, stomach ailments, and arthritis.

GEMSTONE POWER!

RHODONITE MEDITATION

Filling your lungs with a gorgeous breath, your chest inflates, your heart is full, and you are called to action. You commit to whatever it takes for you to let go of what no longer serves you. Your emotions are in check and balanced. You forgive yourself and anyone who has ever hurt or disappointed you. You pave the way for true friendships, true love, and true passion to enter your realm. You have never been more ready than now. There is no turning back. You feel a confidence that you haven't felt in a long time, and it feels great! You breathe with ease into any situation that arises. You bring order out of chaos. Your arms are open. Your heart is full. You are confident. You remember what you have always known; that you were born ready!

36.
ROSE QUARTZ

Rose Quartz is the stone of the heart. It promotes love, self love, and friendship. It is a soothing and gentle stone which allows you to instantly feel calm, relaxed, and peaceful. It is a stone of angelic connections. Rose quartz is helpful to those who wish to bring in romantic love, or to heal a broken heart. It can help with self confidence and self esteem. It is a stone of beauty. Rose quartz shares its sensual qualities with the owner, and aids in the areas of the heart, blood circulation, sexual issues, and fertility. It is recommended to always keep a chunk of Rose Quartz (and Amazonite) near your computer or electronics to balance out the energy. Rose quartz is pink in color, ranging from very pale to deeper hues. If you are looking for a way to make amends with someone you've had a falling out with, consider rose quartz as a peacemaking gift. It is very popular in all types of jewelry, as its calming effects are notorious.

ROSE QUARTZ MEDITATION

You feel so peaceful and calm, you are almost dreamy. With every breath, your heart opens up more and more. Opening up to the possibility of new love for yourself or another. You feel safe and secure knowing your angels are working in your favor. The day is fresh, and there is a sense of peace between you and those from your past, present, and future. You honor forgiveness and feel your heart grow even more. Calm and peaceful. Dreamy. You are in a state of perfection where everyone and everything supports you. You feel fertile and can sense the love growing inside of you. Cultivating a beautiful foundation for all that is good and serving you in the highest way. You have love, friendship, romance, passion, and the purest kind of joy. You speak honestly and truthfully and directly from your heart. Your heart knows all. Your heart knows you. Your heart is the key to the highest forms of love. You have unlocked the door. You are complete.

37.
RUBY

Ruby is an intense stone and an activator of the Root Chakra at the base of the spine. This red stone increases life force, passion, vibrancy, commitment, good health, and orgasmic sexual activity. When blood circulation increases, general health improves especially in the spleen and intestinal area. Ruby helps with just that. It is an action activator, and a chosen stone for Leaders and Kings. It can help you put aside any sense of insecurity so you can rise to greatness with ease. It has been known to cut recovery time in half after a health ailment or surgery. This is a stone of taking charge. It is ruled by Mars, and the sign Aries, and is synonymous with passion, great ideas, action, and success.

RUBY MEDITATION

You are ready! You have never been more ready than you are right now! You feel strong and can take charge with ease. You are smart and your strategy is in place. You are a leader; comfortable in your own skin and confident with your plans. Your goals are mapped out, and you are ready to take action. The energy is intense, and you unleash a wild streak that becomes you. Your cheeks are flushed. You feel passionate about your life and your body. You feel strong and sexy. Everyone notices this shift. You are embracing life like never before. Every minute is delicious, and you are hungry for more. You are empowered and empowering. You are vibrant. You are passionate. You are strong. You are confident. You are one step ahead of everyone else. You are a winner!

38.
SAPPHIRE

Sapphire is a stone of loyalty and faithfulness. It is a brilliant blue color and possesses the power to support straightforward communication. When you think of sapphire, think of the phrase "true blue." It is said that Moses received the Ten Commandments on tablets made of sapphire, making this a very sacred stone. It promotes wisdom, faith and knowledge, and can help alleviate pain, reduce fevers, and promote sobriety. Sapphires are divine stones often found in royalty. Princess Diana's sapphire engagement ring is among one of the most famous of all time. The stone often boasts a beautiful star increasing its magical capabilities and worth. This September birthstone can help heal depression and anxiety, and along with agate, is the official state gem of Montana.

SAPPHIRE MEDITATION

Focus on the star and be transported to another time and place where you are surrounded by your Royal Court. You are loved and revered by many. You are a loyal servant, king, and wizard. You can create a space of truth that is never questioned. Your word is true blue. You are honest, faithful, loyal, and loving. Your head is held high and you walk with strength and ease. You can communicate effortlessly and everyone listens. Your word is golden. As you return to your present awareness, you incorporate these similar feelings. You are a loving leader, and mesmerizing communicator. You speak the truth, and you are heard. You are loyal and faithful, and you are loved. Dearly, dearly loved. You speak from your heart, and you create magical truths. You are a weaver of eternal wisdom.

39.
SELENITE

Selenite is a beautiful white stone with a cat's eye sheen. There is a magical quality to its shimmer and shine. It can be smooth and polished into a sphere or an oval, or remain in its natural formation like a tower. Some selenite towers are made into table lamps making their glow even more magical, energetic, and powerful. Selenite is a calming and soothing stone that attracts the angelic realm into your life for guidance and answers to your prayers. It can amp up the energy of other stones in your collection, as well as facilitate reconciliations within fractured relationships. Many healers rely on selenite wands to unblock energy and bring in peace and security. Used during meditation, selenite can bring in clarity through calm introspection.

SELENITE MEDITATION

The light is on. The light inside of you. Your angelic team responds to your light and answers your prayers. You are safe and secure. Breathing in peacefulness and calm. Your edges are softening. You begin to glow. The pieces of your life that no longer serve you simply melt away. You are breathing. You are light. You are at peace. There is no illness. There is no fear. There is only you and those who support you. Your angels shower you with love, and your inner light responds by getting brighter and brighter. Everything and everyone around you is affected. No more feuds. No more fractures. Simply peace, calm, and the knowing that you are protected and loved and connected to the ALL.

40.
SHIVA LINGAM

Shiva Lingams are egg shaped stones found in one of the seven sacred sites of India, the Narmada River in Onkar Mandhata. The villagers polish the stones to make them shine, though many utilize the stones in their organic state. They represent fertility and is a phallic symbol for God Shiva. The egg is the symbol for all creation, birth, and life. These stones help to create the perfect balance between your male and female qualities, and resonate to all four elements; earth, air, water, and fire. It can activate the kundalini (life force) in your Root Chakra for a burst of energy, as well as align your entire chakra system. Shiva Lingams can be used to fight impotence and infertility, and strengthen and balance the yin and yang in your entire body.

SHIVA LINGAM MEDITATION

You feel infinite. There is no beginning and no end. You are birth and life. You are earth, air, water, and fire. You are everything. You are the circle of life, fertility, and hope. You are energy and knowledge and power. You are the breath of life. You are passion and love. You are strong, energetic, and completely balanced. You are yin and yang, male and female. You are the seasons, the cycles, the ALL. You are whole. You are present. You are aligned. Your chakras open, open, open, like lotus blossoms blooming. They are vibrant in color; red, orange, yellow, green, blue, indigo, and violet. A spectrum of light and love. You embrace life. You are life. You are complete. You are ONE.

41.
SMOKY QUARTZ

Smoky Quartz is a clear stone that is usually light to dark brown. It encourages tolerance, protection, and the ability to cope during difficult times. Smoky quartz can help reduce stress while alleviating backaches, cramps, pain, and nervousness. It is a powerful stone that allows you to make wise purchases and handle money efficiently. It can unblock what is stuck so creativity can flow once again. Smoky quartz can transform negative energy, and help you to focus. It can clear up aches and pains, and bring about peace of mind. This stone has staying power as it shifts your energy from the outworn to the new. In regards to achieving unity in all types of relationships and cooperation in groups, smoky quartz is an excellent choice. This powerhouse is the official state gem of New Hampshire.

SMOKY QUARTZ MEDITATION

You are ready for an epiphany. You are ready to leave behind the outworn and old ways of thinking. You are no longer distracted by what others say or do. You are sure of who you are and your purpose. As you meditate on this concept, you feel the clarity and focus roll in slowly and understand that your future is being anchored into place. You creative juices are flowing. You can sense a certain amount of excitement. You are able to achieve balance and unity with all those who serve you well in life. You feel healthy and strong; limber and lithe. You feel younger than you have in years. The pain and hardships of the past are drifting away on life preservers you no longer need. You are ready to release the ropes once and for all. You are ready. You are able. You are strong. You are focused. You are in control of your life, and it feels good, feels grand, as you finally...let...it...all...go.

42.
SNOWFLAKE
OBSIDIAN

Snowflake Obsidian is a wonderful example of nature's beauty. It is a black stone with white snowflakes laced throughout. Just like its obsidian cousin, it provides spiritual protection, and helps to remove energy blockages. It dissolves fear, and emotional trauma. As it balances your chakra system, it can help you find the truth within yourself. Snowflake Obsidian can accelerate wound healing and decrease hardening of the arteries by increasing blood circulation. It also helps to warm your hands and feet. Snowflake obsidian can be held during meditation and when asking for guidance, the information will flow right in. It helps to overcome obstacles, find solutions to life's problems, and open the way for you to become the absolute best you can be.

SNOWFLAKE OBSIDIAN MEDITATION

You are no longer afraid. The past means nothing. Any emotional or mental connections to pain and sadness are released. You can feel your blood pumping strongly from your heart center and flowing throughout your body. This is comforting, energizing, and exhilarating. You feel warm and secure. There are no obstacles, only successes. Problems that once seemed overwhelming diminish before your very eyes. You are confident and in control. There is no fear, only possibilities. An endless stream of undying truths that have been hidden far too long come rushing to the forefront. You see yourself as if for the first time. In perfect harmony with your surroundings and the people that fill it. You feel confidence, and it exudes from your pores. Decisions are made in a snap. You have left fear behind. You see clearly. You are capable. You achieve success. You are ready.

43.
SODALITE

Sodalite is a dark blue stone with white inclusions. It is often mistaken for Lapis Lazuli. Sodalite promotes honesty and assuages guilt. It helps to gain insight, clarity, and vision. Intuition is sharpened, and the mind chatter is calmed. It helps to teach you to become more rational and logical. Sodalite aids healing in the fifth chakra areas of the throat, larynx, vocal chords, and thyroid. It is a stone that enhances writing abilities and communication through the written word. Athletes use it for endurance. It quiets the mind and puts forth a logical vision of what can be. It is a calming stone that brings peace to you and your living environment.

SODALITE MEDITATION

Ah, finally...peace. Your mind is quiet. Peaceful. Still. The idle mind chatter has ceased. You can think without interruption. You know what to say and how to say it. Your thoughts are clear, focused, and concise. You are easily understood. Your thoughts come forth in perfect timing and you are motivated to write them down. First in a journal, and then in a letter. You can say what you want, and the words flow effortlessly. You are exercising a muscle that has longed to be flexed. Your throat is relaxed, and communication flows freely. You can breathe, and you feel peaceful. Tapping into your intuition, you learn to trust the thoughts that come through your head. They are positive and loving. There is no judgement, only approval, for you, your loved ones, and the environment. Breathe. You are finally at peace.

44.
SUGILITE

Sugilite is a very rare and important stone. It is a stone supported by Archangel Michael as it clears the way for your human side to embrace your spiritual connection. This is a love stone. Combine it with amethyst to connect to a deeper spiritual path, or with hematite to ground in your human desires. This stone will protect you, and foster a luminescent glow to your aura. It cleanses the chakras and aligns you to your true purpose. Use it to alleviate headaches and disharmony. Sugilite helps to clear the path for forgiveness, and pave the way for a truly honest existence. It's a loving stone. A protective stone. A cleansing stone. It's startling purple hues feel otherworldly. Connect to the angelic realm with this one.

SUGILITE MEDITATION

You will notice the shift immediately. As the top of your Crown Chakra lifts open like a moon roof on your vehicle. You are wide open and receiving all the loving kindness from above. The angels are smiling, and Archangel Michael's wingspan wraps around you with ease. You step into another world, a safe place, where you are connected to God and Spirit and the Divine. You are filled with warmth and protection as you vow to do your life's work in the best way possible. The angels smile on you and nod in agreement. You connect with the earth to make sure your feet are still on the ground. You understand the partnership between earth and sky, spirit and intention. You vow to be the best that you can be, and your angels and spirit guides agree. You are supported, loved, and protected. And you will never, ever, feel alone again.

45.
SUNSTONE

Sunstone is a brownish orange stone with a sparkle that catches in the light. It was a stone once favored by wizards and soothsayers for its iridescence and magical qualities. It promotes leadership, self worth, good luck, and optimism. All the characteristics of the sign of Leo, which is ruled by the Sun. Sunstone can stimulate self-healing, and is a wonderful anti-depressant. Just being around it can make you feel better! Many believe that lighting a white candle and placing sunstone before it will bring protective light and radiance to your home. Utilizing it with its counterpart, Moonstone, will help you balance your own personal yin and yang. This stunning stone supports the Solar Plexus Chakra, and helps to fire up a draining life force. Placing it on the center of your body while lying down can add a luster to your energetic field that might be in need of a boost. Sunstone, which is high in energy and vitality, is the official state gem of Oregon.

SUNSTONE MEDITATION

The warmth fills you from the inside out. You are glowing in the center of your body as your solar plexus fills with light. It beams brighter and brighter as your energy increases to embrace the day. You recognize your true self worth and are immediately lifted up, smiling, to shine like the sun. Your optimism is contagious as you reach out and spread your loving light to friends, strangers, co-workers, and associates. You are recognized for your leadership abilities as you engage in fairness and positivity. You are sending a permanent message to your subconscious mind that YES, you are lucky, and the world is a brighter and better place because you are in it. You are joyful. You are positive. You are optimistic. Your touch is golden. You are shining.

46.
TEKTITE/MOLDAVITE

Tektite and moldavite are the only stones that are really out of this world. Moldavite came to earth via a meteor nearly 15 million years ago, and landed in what is now the Czech Republic. All moldavite stones are tektite, but not all tektites are moldavite. Moldavite is very rare, very powerful, and can be used to catapult you to new awareness, better health, and a higher vibration of being. They look opaque but held up to the light are transparent. Many healers choose moldavite as their talisman, as the healing qualities of the stones align with fifth dimensional frequencies. They are known to speed things up in such areas as career, reputation, and life direction. Many people have marveled that moldavite, which is part of the tektite family, has led to spontaneous physical and emotional healings. Moldavite was not discovered until 1985, and since then has gone on to become a powerful force in the gemstone and healing world. This stone, which literally has fallen from the sky, allows for healing to take place where it is most needed on all four levels of your being; physical, emotional, mental, and spiritual. Tektite is black and though energetic, is not as transformational as its moldavite offspring.

TEKTITE/MOLDAVITE
MEDITATION

It's like nothing you have ever felt before. Is it a buzz? A vibration? You notice that you feel different, like passing through doorways into another dimension. The feelings are quick and fleeting. You are fully aware that your life path is shifting. You might be headed into a new direction, or reassured that you are on the right track. You feel calmer, and release past trauma and fears. You feel excited knowing that your physical health is shifting into a higher gear. Your energy is palatable as you embrace the notion that something spectacular is occurring. You connect with sound and vibration, color and dimensions. Your consciousness expands two fold, three fold, and more. You understand that this is a gift from the universe, and you receive it with dignity and aplomb. You are buzzing with excitement, as your life unfolds spectacularly. You are living your life's purpose in the best of health and circumstances. You are upgraded into the best that you can be.

47.
TIGERS EYE

Tiger's Eye is a golden brown stone with a magical quality that is undeniable. It is a stone that is associated with the mind and allows you to see beyond the scope of your physical vision. It's a lucky stone, and is often a gift for those starting a new venture. The eye of the tiger means you can see all, and this stone enhances that ability. It promotes balance, and offers strength to get through difficult times. Since it helps to alleviate doubt, Tiger's Eye can be an effective tool for decision making. It is a creative stone that offers vision and clarity. If you are in the midst of changes in your life, Tiger's Eye can help ground you and allow you to see what you most need to do to succeed. It is connected to the earth, and for many, is a calming stone during meditation. Tiger's Eye enhances the Third Eye Chakra, as well as support your solar plexus and life force.

TIGER'S EYE MEDITATION

Your Third Eye clicks open. Wide. You see in silence. Like a tiger in the jungle. You assess the situation, and tune in to your surroundings. You are all knowing. All seeing. In the midst of a challenge, you are calm and focused. You know what to do, and how to handle it. You approach all situations with caution, so as not to throw anyone off track. Your focus is on the task at hand. You are in control. You are calm. Your insights are on target. As you move forth on your path's direction, you feel the earth move stealthily underfoot. You move towards your goal. You manifest a perfect scenario for achievement. You have planned well. You succeed. You reign supreme. You have averted the crisis. You are calm. You are satisfied. You are proud.

48.
TOPAZ

Topaz is the "Wishes Come True" stone connecting you to the Angelic Realm. It promotes wisdom, honesty, and awakens the part of you that wants to achieve your dreams. Energy flow is stimulated, eating disorders can be conquered, and metabolism and nervous disorders are balanced. Topaz is the color of the sky - clear or light blue, and brown like a rainy day. This November birthstone opens the way for karmic debt to be paid, and can clear away stale and stagnant energy once and for all. It allows you to tap into your consciousness for what serves you best in all areas of your life. It helps purify your emotions as well as your actions. Texas and Utah have adopted this multi-dimensional stone as their official state gem.

TOPAZ MEDITATION

Make a wish. Don't stop at just one. Make more. Make as many wishes as you want. The skies may have been gray and cloudy, but they are a brilliant blue now. Your wishes take shape and glisten in the sun. Bright, shiny wishes that are yours for the taking. Your angels are smiling on you now as they pluck each wish from your subconscious and unwrap it with glee. They conspire to manifest your dreams and goals in magical ways. You are karmically free to proceed. The wheels of energy inside your body begin to move. Slowly at first, and then faster and faster. You are picking up speed on your path to achievement. Your health is aligned with your goals, your body is in sync with the foods you eat, and you are more awake than you've ever been. With the support of your angelic team, you are ready for victory. Wish after wish, like touchdown after touchdown, is made in perfect sequence. It's a perfect day. A perfect life. And you, are perfect in it.

49.
TOURMALINE

Tourmaline is a force to be reckoned with. It's a powerful healing stone that comes in an assortment of chakra colors including pinks and greens and what looks like black, but held up to the light is a color unto itself. It combines spirituality with protection, soul awareness with intellect, and attunes your body into one harmonious whole. It provides strength, creativity, love, truth, sensitivity, caring, inner peace, commitment, and purification of one's self. Tourmaline reminds you that you are a light being in a physical body, and helps access pertinent information for the Greater Good. It can help your inner child heal a broken heart from episodes of abuse, and turn negative energy into positive. It inspires confidence and courage, and when placed on the body over the corresponding chakra, will completely balance you for greater health and well-being. It cleanses the blood, helps overcome fertility, and speeds up the healing process from burns. Tourmaline can also be used to alleviate constipation and lower back pain. This official state gem of Maine is a prize.

TOURMALINE MEDITATION

Your body is ready to receive the powerful energy from Source. From chakra to chakra, you will first feel cleansed and then energized as your vibrational flow increases. From the base of your spine to the top of your head, you feel grounded, stable, and practical. Stiffness disappears and you are able to move with ease. You release any blockages and pave the way for fertile and creative endeavors to grow. You feel joyous, and may be prone to laughing. Your sense of self is heightened, and your mind expands in consciousness. You feel invigorated, renewed, and overwhelmed with a sense of compassion. Your heart beats stronger as you embrace the feeling of connectedness and oneness. You are communicative and psychic, intuitive and deep. You revel in knowledge and universal truths. You are prosperous and abundant. You are smart and protected. You are connected to Spirit. You are part of the ALL THAT IS, and you are glorious.

50.
TURQUOISE

Turquoise is an artist's stone promoting creativity and self expression. It helps to connect to one's muse as it takes intuition and inspiration to new levels. It is a stone of friendship and if given as a gift will offer protection and positivity. Turquoise can bring good luck, foresight, spiritual grounding, and is a mood balancer. It aids healing in the areas of acid vs. alkaline, stomach and gout problems, and helps to fight against viral infections. It also creates warmth, and relaxes cramps. This December birthstone brings about peace of mind, loyalty and enhances the throat chakra. It is loved by many especially those in Arizona, Nevada, and New Mexico who claim turquoise as their official state gem.

TURQUOISE MEDITATION

Your breath and heart rate become one as you connect with your inner shaman. An amulet around your neck brings you peace and protection. You are an artist and creator of your life. You are intuitive about color and light and herbs and tinctures. You are a free spirit who can transport easily between worlds. You see an eagle and understand the eagle is also you. You are at one with your people, and you offer protection and guidance. Your gifts are many as you paint a world that is rich in color and textures. You understand the essence of goodness as it is bestowed on you through friendships and culture. You run along the river of luck as it takes you to fertile pastures. From there you create a vivid world of color and light, insight, and loyalty. You speak the truth and the world listens. You are inspired. You are inspiring.

51.
UNAKITE

Unakite celebrates the Divine Feminine. It is a beautiful green and salmon stone that helps you to balance your emotional body. Utilizing unakite to connect to your Higher Self can help to release burdens that no longer serve you, so you can move forward in your life with ease. Unakite aids healing in the areas of the reproductive system, stimulating healthy pregnancies. It is ruled by the sign of Cancer, and supports the heart and sacral chakras. Unikite stems from the word 'unity' and means growing together. It will help you to connect to your emotional side so that you may grow a life that is healthy, happy, and can serve you in the best way. Use unakite for awakening the life inside of you that has been dormant. It is a symbol of birth and rebirth.

UNAKITE MEDITATION

You feel reborn. As if you have given birth to a new you. A better you. A kinder you. A new and improved you. You are excited about life's possibilities. You feel secure and supported and nurtured. And in return, you support and nurture those around you. Your arms are open and you are ready to receive. To receive love. To receive joy. To receive abundance. You have given birth to a new you and you are eager to venture forth in the world. Spreading light and love and compassion to all you meet. You see things with fresh eyes, and they are full of wonder. Your heart is open. Your creativity is flowing. You experience the joys and pleasures of life as if for the first time. Through a baby's eyes, you can see what you have never fully seen before. A life of love and support, and the understanding that you are never, ever alone. Embrace the child inside of you. You are safe. You are nurtured. You are a NEW you.

52.
ZIRCON

Zircon comes in a variety of colors including red, orange, brown, yellow, and even clear. It helps to open all the chakras to a higher vibration, especially enhancing your sixth sense of sight. Intuition and clairvoyance are heightened, and dreams become more lucid. Zircon may help to lift depression and overcome sadness that comes with loss. It releases fear and opens the way for detoxification of the liver. Menstrual cramps may also be subdued. Zircon is associated with the sign of Capricorn; a strong stone for a strong sign. It symbolizes that out of the darkness comes the light, and that the darkest hour comes just before the dawn. It reminds you to stay hopeful as it releases material connections and paves the way for a more spiritual understanding.

GEMSTONE POWER!

ZIRCON MEDITATION

You have traveled far, and can see the light at the end of the tunnel. There is no turning back. Your past is over, and the future awaits. The fog has lifted, and you can see for miles. The future is bright, and you embrace the responsibility of living a life that is perfect for you. Tears have dried, guilt is released. There is nothing to go back to. You have been completely reborn and transported to the right path. The perfect path. One by one your chakras light up like traffic lights, giving you the go ahead to have a brilliant life. One that is rich with opportunity and joy, experience and luck. Your intuition triggers insights with ease, and you can easily navigate your way from this point on. You have clarity and focus, and feel balanced and sure. You are completely calm in your choices, and solid on your feet. You have traveled a long way and the road was hard, but the past is over, and you are at peace. This is a new beginning. Welcome to your new life.

CARING FOR YOUR GEMSTONES

Your gemstones are alive, and vibrate in conjunction with your energy field. Because of this, they take on the energy that exudes from your emotional and physical body. Citrine and kyanite are two gemstones that have the ability to reject negativity so they don't need to be cleaned or cleared, but mostly all other gemstones require some clearing and cleaning so they can serve you in the best way.

Your gemstones form a tight relationship with you and can absorb your sadness, pain, and suffering. However, even your gemstones can max out and only be able to take so much before they stop working their magic. Here are some ways to clean and clear your gemstones so they won't get clogged up and sluggish.

1) Gemstones love to be rinsed off under a faucet. Shower your gemstones regularly with cool water, and dry with a soft cloth. This simple act can make even your citrine and kyanite feel happier.

2) Soak your gemstones in a mixture of water and sea salt. If you live near or visit the beach, bring back a jar of salt water. Dry your gemstones in indirect sunlight or an open window. Your gemstones will feel lighter as the old energy drifts away.

3) Put your gemstones in the light of the full moon. While

there, release what no longer serves you. A full moon signifies endings, and is a perfect time to clear your gems.

4) During a New Moon, place your gemstones on a piece of paper with your wishes written on it. A New Moon is a time of new beginnings. Your gemstones will be programmed for your greatest and highest good.

5) If your gemstones are for your personal use, keep them in a soft pouch or wrapped in silk or satin. Keep them close to you. Many keep them on their nightstand, and some sleep with stones under their pillow. It's important to remember that if your stones are for your personal use, no one else should touch them.

6) You can clear your gemstones by burning sage and saying a prayer or blessing while holding them. Release the negativity and replace it with positivity, kindness, good health and well-being. Your words are powerful and your gemstones will respond to them. Remember when releasing energy, always replace it. You don't want to risk opening the way for nothingness.

Allow your gemstone collection to grow organically. Notice what stones you are drawn to before studying their definitions. Gemstones tend to find their owners. Let them find you! Your gemstones will serve you very well. They will protect you, guide you, open the way for clearer channeling, and give you strength. A little soak in some sea salt and water and a little sunshine every now and then is a great treat. Make sure, however, that your stone likes the sun. Some stones, including amethyst, can fade in color if left outside.

NOTES

_____

_____

_____

_____

_____

_____

_____

_____

_____

GEMSTONE POWER!

NOTES

ABOUT THE AUTHOR

Harriette Knight is a Master Healer, Psychic-Medium, Author, and Host of *Harriette Knight's Psychic & Healing Hour* radio show. Her positive outlook on life and intuitive abilities have helped many people learn how to live a fuller and more purposeful life. She is a motivating speaker who through radio broadcasts, lectures, and workshops helps to enlighten others about their chakras and how to reclaim their personal power through balance and intuition.

Harriette Knight is the author of *CHAKRA POWER! How to Fire Up Your Energy Centers to Live a Fuller Life,* and a variety of courses available through Daily OM.com. She shares her wealth of knowledge each week on *Harriette Knight's Psychic & Healing Hour* on Blog Talk Radio discussing metaphysical topics and answering psychic questions from callers. Harriette's Reconnective Healing practice boasts clients from around the world with many commenting that their lives were infinitely changed, and the psychic messages astonishingly accurate. When she is not doing healing sessions and readings, Harriette designs a line of healing jewelry for her company, Charity Clarity Jewelry. All the jewelry is one-of-a-kind and infused with healing energy. A portion of the proceeds is donated to charity.